ROAD TRIP
JOURNAL

Everything in life is someplace else,
and you get there in a car.

E. B. White

CHRONICLE BOOKS
SAN FRANCISCO

Copyright © 1997 by Chronicle Books.

All rights reserved.
No part of this book may be
reproduced in any form
without written permission
from the publisher.

Printed in Hong Kong
Art Direction: Michael Mabry, Liz Miranda-Roberts
Design: Michael Mabry Design
Text: Jody Trock Stevens

ISBN: 0-8118-1601-X

Distributed in Canada
by Raincoast Books
8680 Cambie Street
Vancouver, B.C. V6P 6M9

10 9 8 7 6 5 4 3 2

Chronicle Books
85 Second Street
San Francisco, CA 94105

www.chronbooks.com

Unless noted otherwise, all of the illustrations and
photographs in *Road Trip Journal* are © M. K. Mabry.

Endsheet art from the postcard collection of John
Baeder, used by permission.

The following images are courtesy of CSA Archive:
AAA Motel, pages 8, 49, and 77; Listening to Tunes,
pages 15, 34, and 83; Man at Gas Pump, pages 17,
59, 113; Bellhop, pages 17, 22, and 71; Clock Car,
pages 26, 85, and 115; Old Car, pages 33, 47, 63,
and 104; Approved Motel, pages 41, 89, and 105;
Landcruiser, pages 50, 91, 111; Looking Both Ways,
pages 57, 107; Man with Gas Nozzle, pages 69, and
93; Driving in the Wind, pages 79, 95.

The map used on pages 1, 7, 12, 18, 25, 31, 36, 43,
49, 54, 61, 67, 72, 79, 84, 90, 97, 102, 108, and 115
is ©1989 by Rand McNally, R.L. 96-S-114.

➡ *ROAD TRIP* IS A JOURNAL FOR THE CAR, THE ULTIMATE VEHICLE OF FREEDOM. RECORD ADVENTURES, RUMINATIONS, AND IMPRESSIONS OF PEOPLE YOU ENCOUNTER AS YOU STEER YOUR MOTION MACHINE DOWN AMERICA'S HIGHWAYS AND BYWAYS. CREATE A MEMORY BOOK OF PARTICULARLY SCENIC ROUTES, THE MOST WELCOMING TOWNS AND CITIES, PLACES YOU HANG YOUR HAT FOR THE NIGHT, FAVORITE REGIONAL CUISINES AND EATERIES THAT FEED YOU WELL, AND EVEN THE BEST-EQUIPPED REST STOPS. ➡ THE PERFECT BLACKTOP COMPANION, *ROAD TRIP* ALSO INCLUDES A VERITABLE TRAVELING MUSIC HIT PARADE TO HELP SELECT TUNES FOR YOUR EXPEDITION, RECOMMENDED WRITINGS FROM OTHER ROAD-TRIPPERS, AND A CHECKLIST OF ESSENTIAL ITEMS THE WELL-PREPARED DRIVER WOULDN'T BE CAUGHT WITHOUT. ➡ YOU CAN MAKE YOUR JOURNAL INTO A ROADWAY SCRAPBOOK BY ADDING PHOTOS, POSTCARDS, AND MEMORABILIA YOU COLLECT ALONG THE WAY: NAPKINS, TICKET STUBS, FLORA AND FAUNA — WHATEVER TREASURES YOU CAN'T LEAVE BEHIND. WHEN YOU LOOK BACK THROUGH ITS PAGES SOMEDAY AND REMINISCE, YOU'LL BE TOOLING DOWN THE INTERSTATE ONCE AGAIN, AWASH IN THE SIGHTS, SOUNDS, AND SMELLS OF YOUR JOURNEY. ➡ DRIVE SAFELY.

	1	2	3	4	5	6	7	8	9	10

DESTINATION   **DATE**

MILEAGE

A

B

C

D

E

F

G

H

I

J

K

L

M

N

O

| 11 | 12 | 13 | 14 | 15 | 16 | 17 | 18 | 19 | 20 |

DESTINATION

DATE

MILEAGE

> **Travel seems not just a way of having a good time, but something that every self-respecting citizen ought to undertake, like a high-fiber diet, say, or a deodorant.**
>
> Jan Morris

DESTINATION January 27 DATE 2002 Sun

MILEAGE

Today I learned something about myself. I learned that I am a beautiful woman and kind and friendly. This in itself is unsettling for some people but I should not feel bad about me because of this. I am journaling now because I need to get my thoughts out of my head so that I can relax.

I need to make a goal list one that is obtainable.

Register for Esthetics School
Complete Physical Therapy
Find a second job
Find a way to sell the truck
Organize Bedrooms
Gather items to sell on EBAY
Spend more time w/ Krix
Prepare for March workshop
Continue to journaling
Sign Sienna up for Gymboree
Read one book a month at least

Mark Colbath (Tabitha, Chris Gabriel) TKDChefAU 407 938 9453
Maki Herr 425 637·3582
P.O. BOX 1010 360 825 1151
Enumclaw, Wa. 98022 206 793 0750

DESTINATION January 28 Wilmette DATE 2002 Mon

MILEAGE

Had lunch w/ Cindy & Greg.
Bit of a sad day for me,
feel like a good cry.
Snowed a lot today.
+ Need to get Kristina into
piano lessons
How do I find what makes
me happy. If it is enter-
taining someway, how do I
make it happen? Looking
forward to seeing the doctors
this week and getting better.
Wish I could get Jess a job
that makes him happy!

	1	2	3	4	5	6	7	8	9	10

A DESTINATION   DATE

MILEAGE

B

C

D

E

F

G

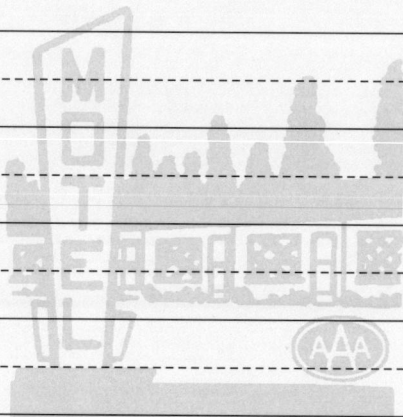

H

I

J

K

L

M

N

O

| 11 | 12 | 13 | 14 | 15 | 16 | 17 | 18 | 19 | 20 |

DESTINATION **DATE**

A

MILEAGE

B

C

D

E

F

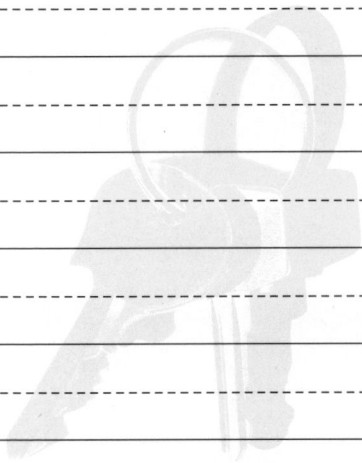

G

H

I

J

K

L

> **Reading about journeys while on a journey is an intensely stimulating experience.**
>
> Umberto Eco

M

N

O

	1	2	3	4	5	6	7	8	9	10

DESTINATION   **DATE**

                                   MILEAGE

DESTINATION

DATE

MILEAGE

A
B
C
D
E
F
G
H
I
J
K
L

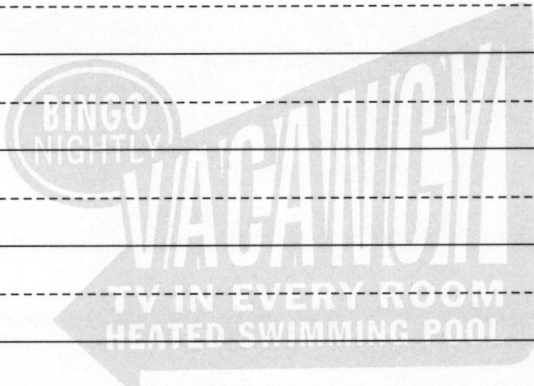

M

Nothing helps scenery like ham and eggs.

Mark Twain

N

O

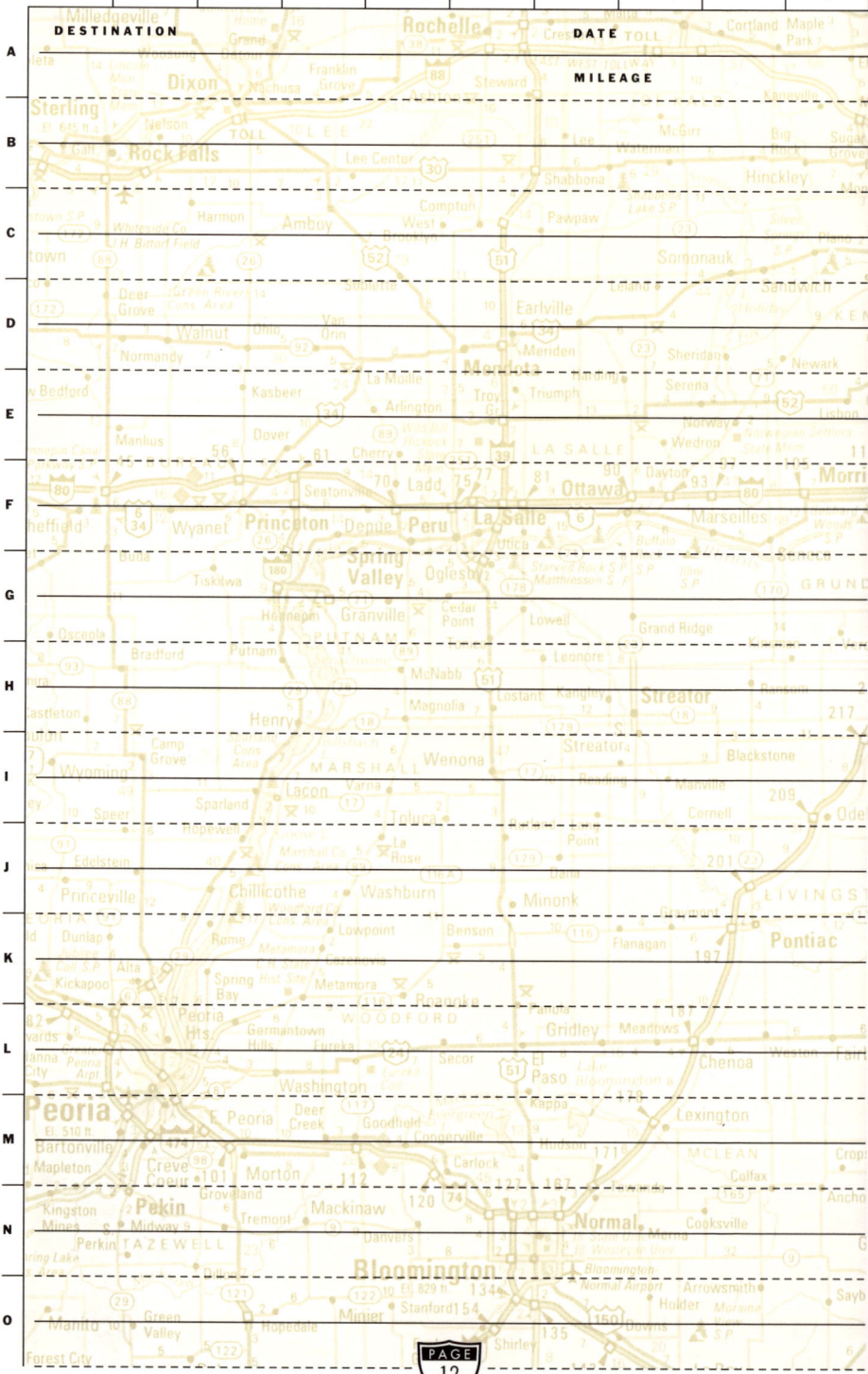

DESTINATION

DATE

MILEAGE

A
B
C
D
E
F
G
H
I
J
K
L

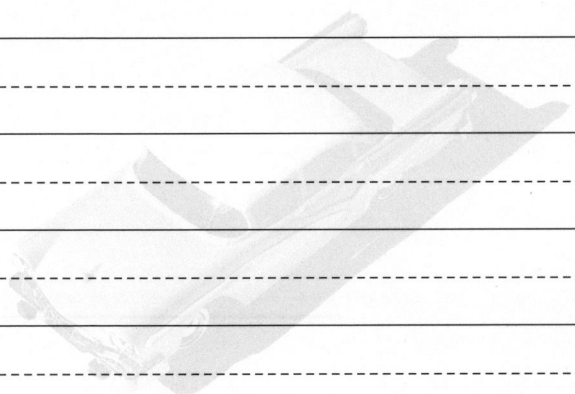

M
N
O

	1	2	3	4	5	6	7	8	9	10

DESTINATION

DATE

MILEAGE

A

B

C

D

E

F

G

H

I

J

K

L

M

N

O

DESTINATION   DATE

MILEAGE

A
B
C
D
E
F
G
H
I

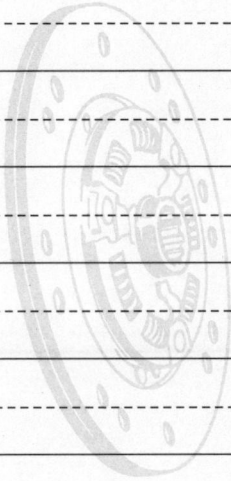

A driver is
a king
on a vinyl
bucket seat
throne,
changing
direction
with the
turn of a
wheel,
changing
the climate
with a
flick of the
button,
changing
the music
with the
switch of
a dial.

Andrew H. Malcolm

DESTINATION

DATE

MILEAGE

DESTINATION   DATE

MILEAGE

**Have a
nice trip,
Dick.**

Betty Ford

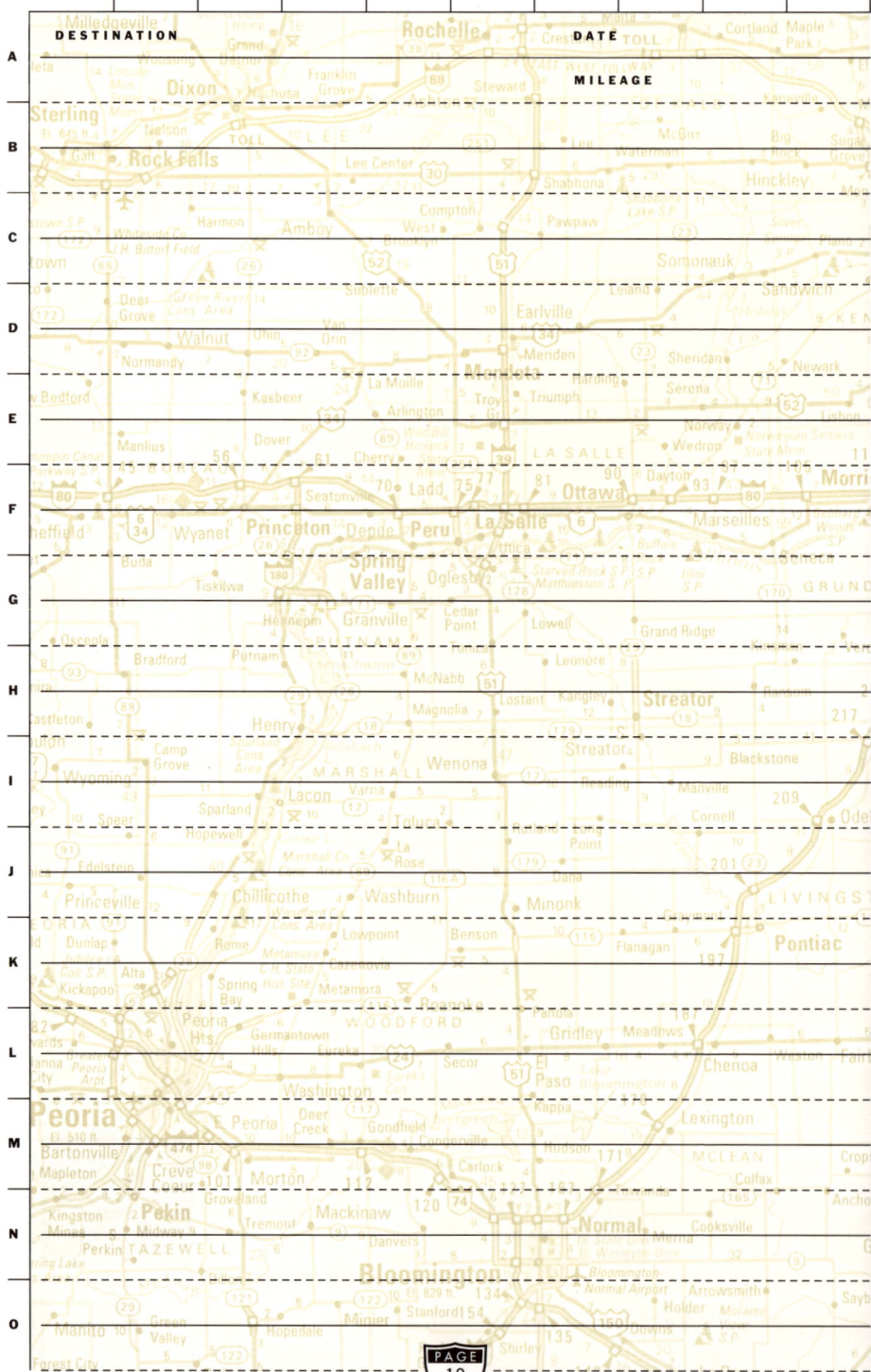

	1	2	3	4	5	6	7	8	9	10
A										
B										
C										
D										
E										
F										
G										
H										
I										
J										
K										
L										
M										
N										
O										

11	12	13	14	15	16	17	18	19	20

DESTINATION   **DATE**

A

                                   MILEAGE

B

C

D

E

F

G

H

I

J

K

> **Eventually
> I realized
> that many
> of the most
> important
> changes in
> my life had
> come
> about
> because of
> my travel
> experiences.**
>
> Michael Crichton

L

M

N

O

	1	2	3	4	5	6	7	8	9	10

DESTINATION **DATE**

MILEAGE

A

B

C

D

E

F

G

H

I

J

K

L

M

N

O

| 11 | 12 | 13 | 14 | 15 | 16 | 17 | 18 | 19 | 20 |

DESTINATION

DATE

MILEAGE

A

B

C

D

E

F

G

H

I

J

	1	2	3	4	5	6	7	8	9	10

A DESTINATION

DATE

MILEAGE

B

C

D

E

F

G

H

I

J

K

L

M

N

O

| 11 | 12 | 13 | 14 | 15 | 16 | 17 | 18 | 19 | 20 |

DESTINATION

DATE

MILEAGE

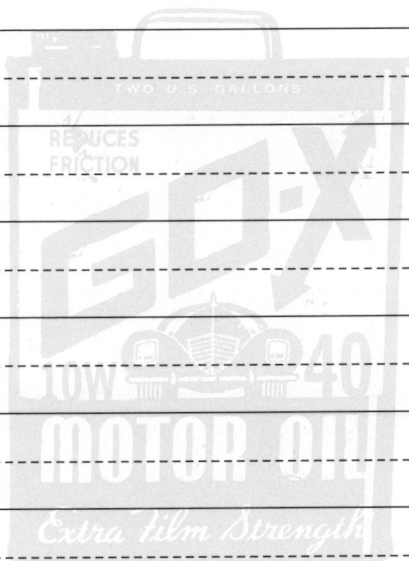

> The real meaning of travel, like that of a conversation by the fireside, is the discovery of oneself through contact with other people.
>
> Paul Tournier

DESTINATION

DATE

MILEAGE

DESTINATION _____ **DATE** _____

MILEAGE _____

	1	2	3	4	5	6	7	8	9	10

DESTINATION **DATE**

MILEAGE

A

B

C

D

E

F

G

H

I

J

K

L

M

N

O

DESTINATION

DATE

MILEAGE

A

B

C

D

E

F

G

H

I

J

K

> You got a
> fast car,
> I want a
> ticket to
> anywhere,
> maybe we
> can make a
> deal,
> maybe
> together
> we can get
> somewhere.
>
> Tracy Chapman

L

M

N

O

	1	2	3	4	5	6	7	8	9	10
A	**DESTINATION**						**DATE**			
							MILEAGE			
B										
C										
D										
E										
F										
G										
H										
I										
J										
K										
L										
M										
N										
O										

DESTINATION

DATE

MILEAGE

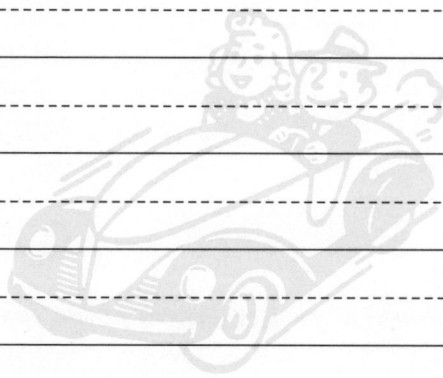

> **Somewhere on the prairie, her thumbs a match for the vastness surrounding her, Sissy Hankshaw Gitche was riffling traffic.**
> **A piece of her was flooded with ecstasy at being free, careening across the continent again.**
>
> Tom Robbins

	1	2	3	4	5	6	7	8	9	10

DESTINATION   **DATE**

MILEAGE

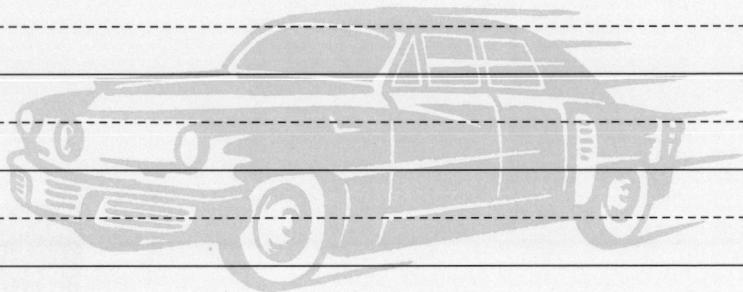

A
B
C
D
E
F
G
H
I
J
K
L
M
N
O

DESTINATION **DATE**

MILEAGE

	1	2	3	4	5	6	7	8	9	10

DESTINATION **DATE**

MILEAGE

A

B

C

D

E

F

G

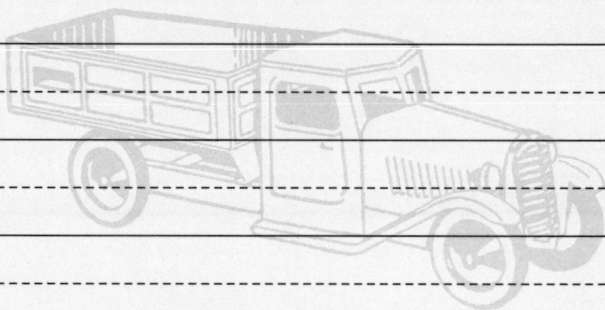

H

I

J

K

L

M

N

O

11 | 12 | 13 | 14 | 15 | 16 | 17 | 18 | 19 | 20

DESTINATION

DATE

MILEAGE

A
B
C
D
E
F
G
H
I
J
K
L

A noisy exhaust almost amounts to a mating call.

J.A. Leavy

M
N
O

	1	2	3	4	5	6	7	8	9	10

A   DESTINATION   DATE

                                         MILEAGE

B

C

D

E

F

G

H

I

J

K

L

M

N

O

DESTINATION

DATE

MILEAGE

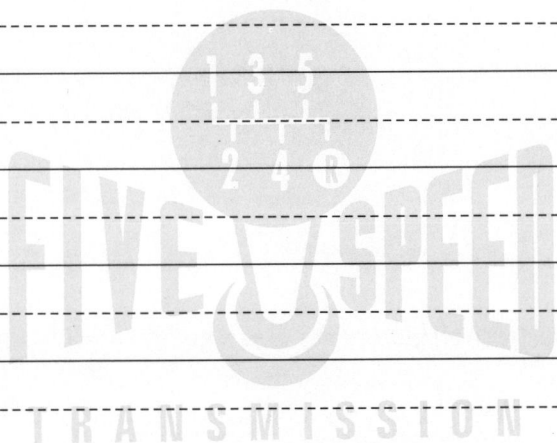

I've got
road maps
from two
dozen
states,
I've got
coast
to coast
just to
contemplate.

Joni Mitchell

DESTINATION

DATE

MILEAGE

A

B

C

D

E

F

G

H

I

J

K

L

M

N

O

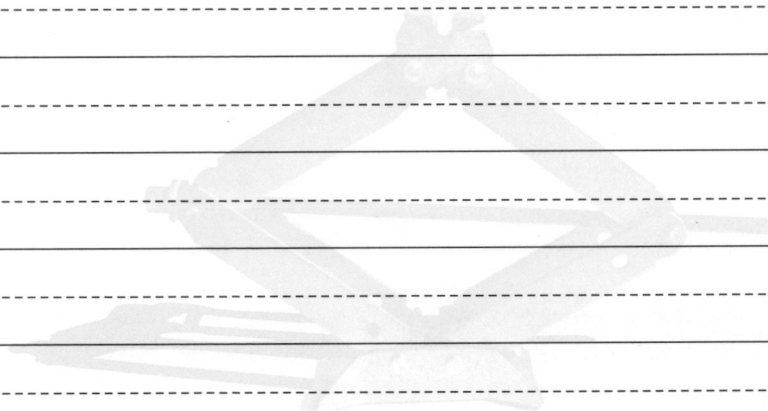

I'm as self-contained as a turtle. When I put my key in the ignition, I have my home right behind me.

Esther Tallamy

	1	2	3	4	5	6	7	8	9	10

DESTINATION   **DATE**

A

                                   MILEAGE

B

C

D

E

F

G

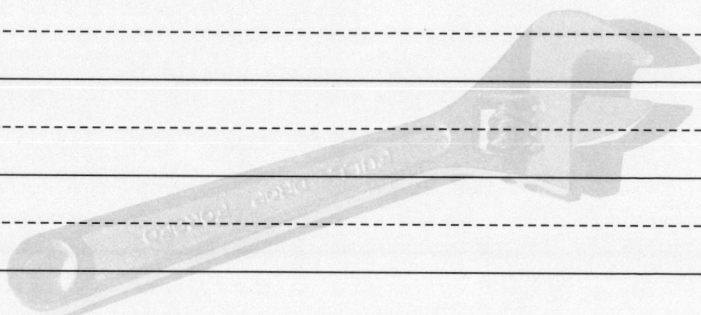

H

I

J

K

L

M

N

O

| 11 | 12 | 13 | 14 | 15 | 16 | 17 | 18 | 19 | 20 |

DESTINATION

DATE

MILEAGE

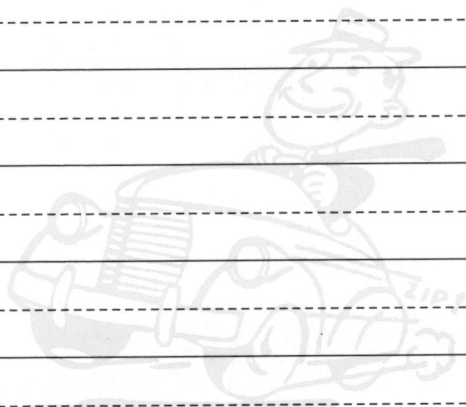

This
continent,
an open
palm
spread
frank
before the
sky.

James Agee

	1	2	3	4	5	6	7	8	9	10

DESTINATION

DATE

MILEAGE

DESTINATION　　　　　　　　　　　　　　　**DATE**

MILEAGE

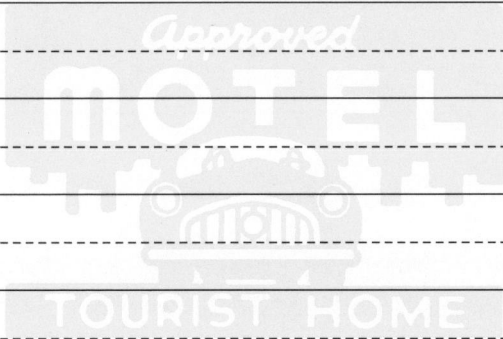

You ain't
been born
til you
get out of
town.

Natalie Merchant

	1	2	3	4	5	6	7	8	9	10

A DESTINATION   DATE

MILEAGE

B

C

D

E

F

G

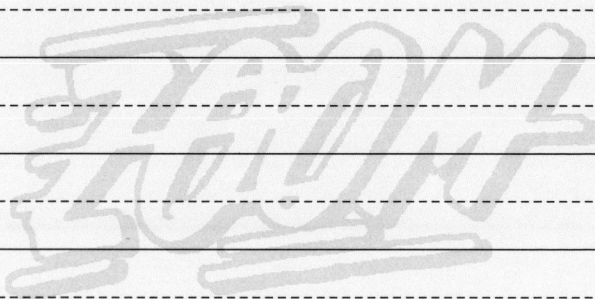

H

I

J

K

L

M

N

O

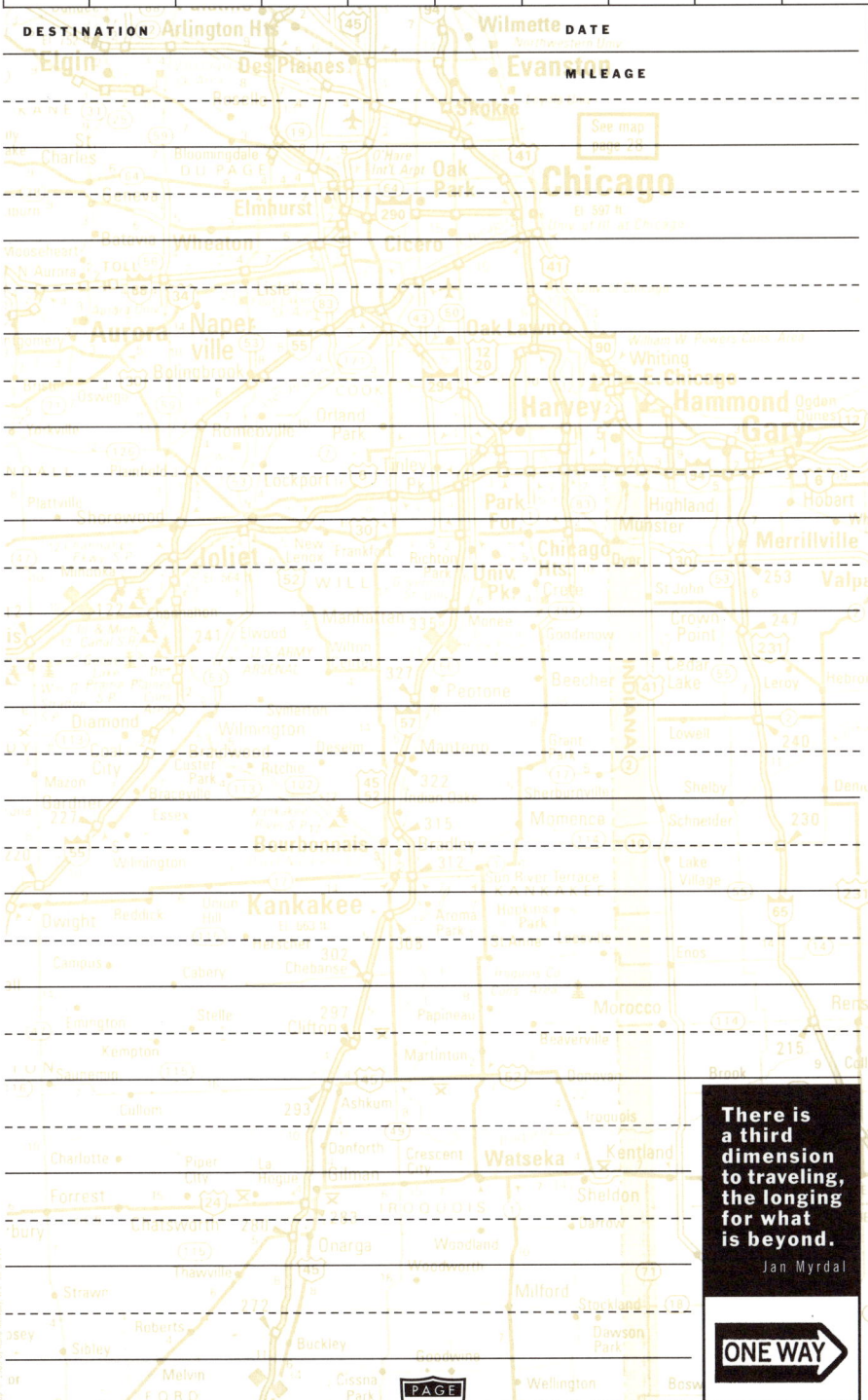

DESTINATION **DATE**

MILEAGE

> There is
> a third
> dimension
> to traveling,
> the longing
> for what
> is beyond.
>
> Jan Myrdal

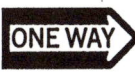
ONE WAY

	1	2	3	4	5	6	7	8	9	10

DESTINATION   **DATE**

A

MILEAGE

B

C

D

E

F

G

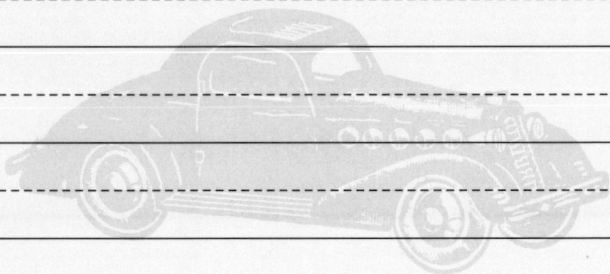

H

I

J

K

L

M

N

O

11	12	13	14	15	16	17	18	19	20

DESTINATION

DATE

MILEAGE

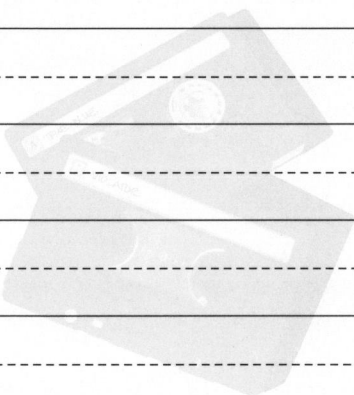

Flat out flatness, the hard line of the horizon. I like the little towns with their handfuls of buildings huddled close to the grain elevators, like medieval towns clustered around their cathedrals.

Gordon Webber

	1	2	3	4	5	6	7	8	9	10

DESTINATION   **DATE**

A

                                   MILEAGE

B

C

D

E

F

G

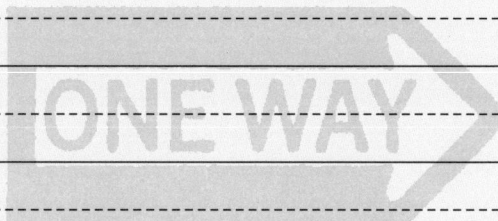

H

I

J

K

L

M

N

O

| 11 | 12 | 13 | 14 | 15 | 16 | 17 | 18 | 19 | 20 |

DESTINATION

DATE

MILEAGE

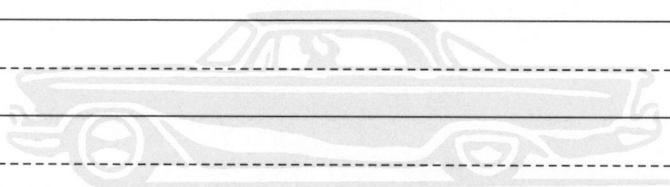

	1	2	3	4	5	6	7	8	9	10

DESTINATION   **DATE**

                                                 MILEAGE

A

B

C

D

E

F

G

H

I

J

K

L

M

N

O

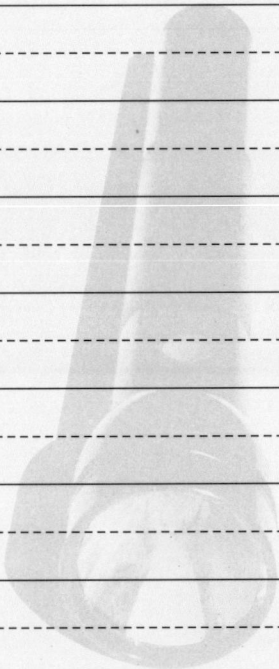

DESTINATION **DATE**

MILEAGE

A

B

C

D

E

F

G

H

I

J

K

L

M

N

O

	1	2	3	4	5	6	7	8	9	10

DESTINATION   **DATE**

MILEAGE

| 11 | 12 | 13 | 14 | 15 | 16 | 17 | 18 | 19 | 20 |

DESTINATION   **DATE**

MILEAGE

A
B
C
D
E
F
G
H
I
J
K

> **O public road, You express me Better than I can express myself.**
>
> Walt Whitman

L
M
N
O

	1	2	3	4	5	6	7	8	9	10

A   DESTINATION   DATE

                                                     MILEAGE

B

C

D

E

F

G

H

I

J

K

L

M

N

O

DESTINATION

DATE

MILEAGE

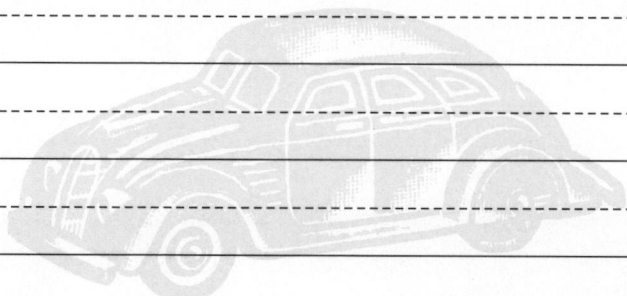

A
B
C
D
E
F
G
H
I
J
K

How does
it feel to
be without
a home,
like a
complete
unknown,
like a
rolling
stone.

Bob Dylan

L
M
N
O

DESTINATION **DATE**

MILEAGE

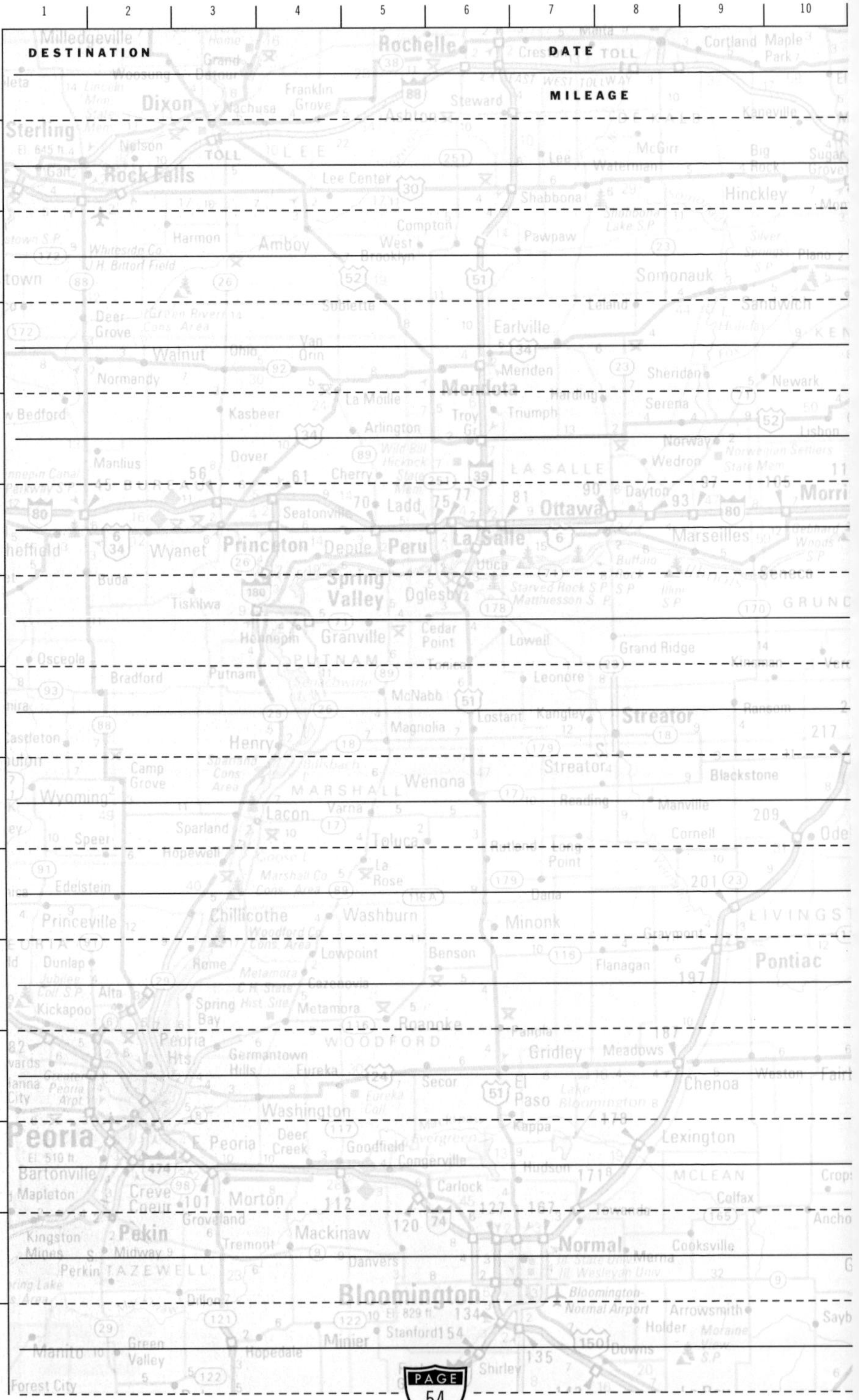

| 11 | 12 | 13 | 14 | 15 | 16 | 17 | 18 | 19 | 20 |

DESTINATION   **DATE**

MILEAGE

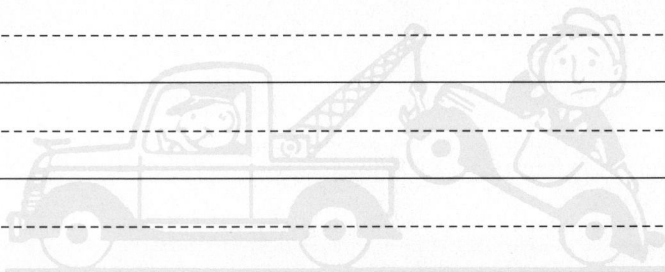

Go
soothingly
on the
greasy
mud, for
therein
lurks the
skid
demon.

Chinese road sign

	1	2	3	4	5	6	7	8	9	10

DESTINATION

DATE

MILEAGE

A
B
C
D
E
F
G
H
I
J
K
L
M
N
O

| 11 | 12 | 13 | 14 | 15 | 16 | 17 | 18 | 19 | 20 |

DESTINATION

DATE

MILEAGE

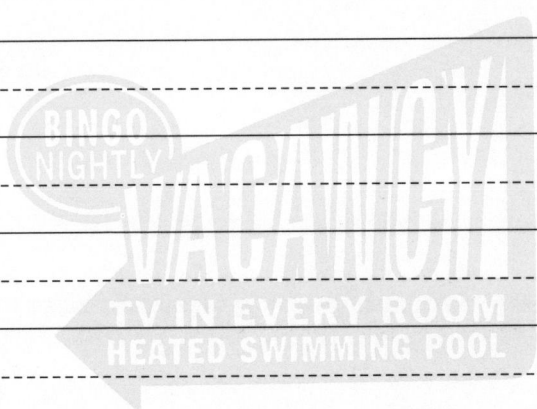

People, when they first come to America, whether as travelers or settlers, become aware of a new and agreeable feeling: that the whole country is their oyster.

Alistair Cooke

	1	2	3	4	5	6	7	8	9	10
A	DESTINATION						DATE			
							MILEAGE			
B										
C										
D										
E										
F										
G										
H										
I										
J										
K										
L										
M										
N										
O										

CRUISE CONTROL

DESTINATION

DATE

MILEAGE

A

B

C

D

E

F

G

H

I

J

K

> For my part, I travel not to go anywhere, but to go. I travel for travel's sake. The great affair is to move.
>
> Robert Louis Stevenson

L

M

N

FREEWAY ENTRANCE

O

	1	2	3	4	5	6	7	8	9	10

DESTINATION   **DATE**

MILEAGE

A

B

C

D

E

F

G

H

I

J

K

L

M

N

O

DESTINATION

DATE

MILEAGE

	1	2	3	4	5	6	7	8	9	10

A DESTINATION

DATE

MILEAGE

B

C

D

E

F

G

H

I

J

K

L

M

N

O

DESTINATION

DATE

MILEAGE

A

B

C

D

E

F

G

H

I

J

K

Down the road in the rain and snow the man and his machine would go, oh the secrets that old car would know.

Marc Cohn

L

M

N

O

DESTINATION

DATE

MILEAGE

| 11 | 12 | 13 | 14 | 15 | 16 | 17 | 18 | 19 | 20 |

DESTINATION　　　　　　　　　　　　　　　　**DATE**

MILEAGE

As one
comes
down the
Henry
Hudson
parkway
along the
river in the
dusk,
New York
is never
real; it
is always
fabulous.

New Yorker

DESTINATION

DATE

MILEAGE

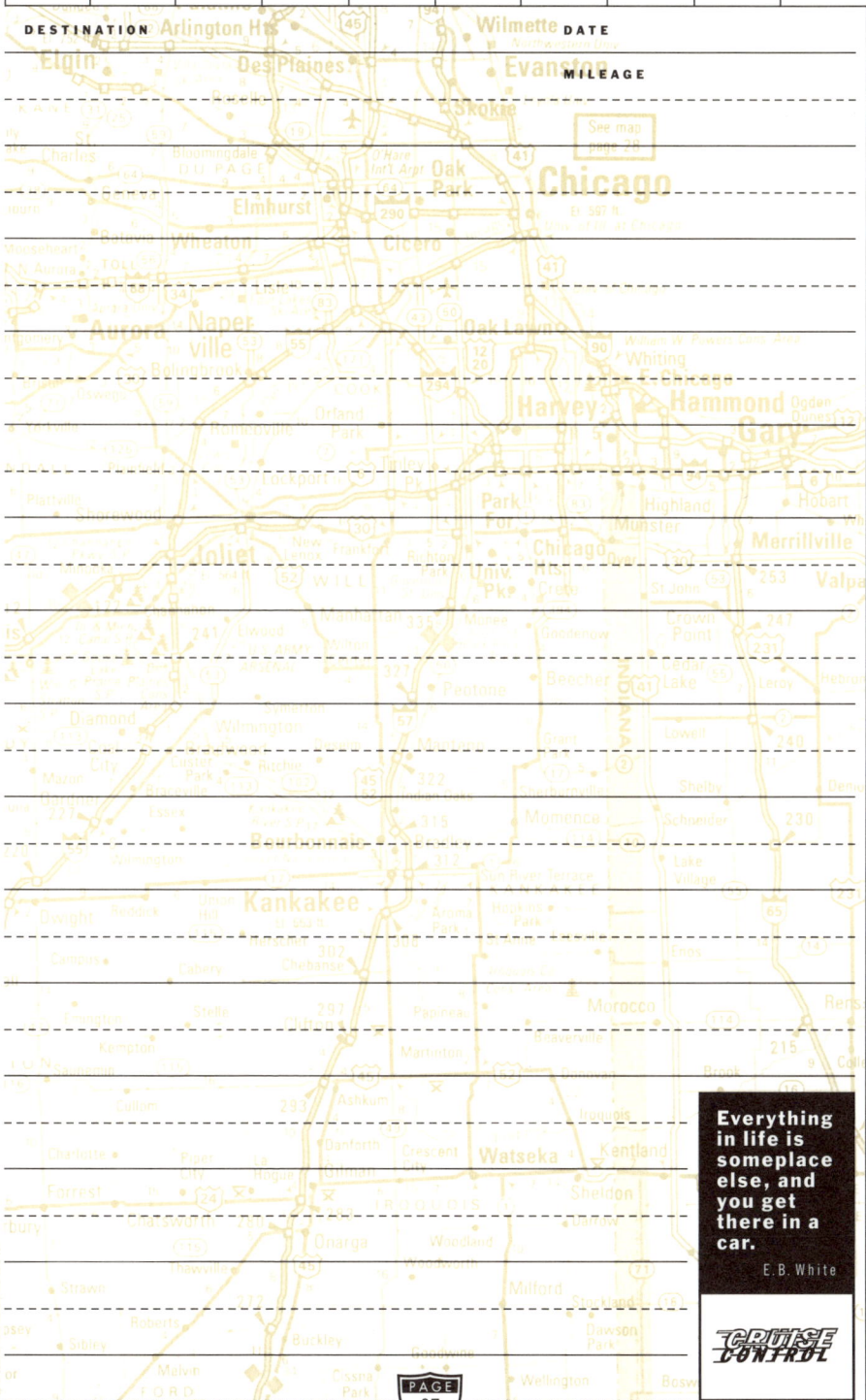

DESTINATION

DATE

MILEAGE

Arlington H.
Wilmette
Northwestern Univ
Elgin
Des Plaines
Evanston
KANE
Skokie
Charles
Bloomingdale
O'Hare
Oak
See map
page 28
DU PAGE
Int'l Arpt.
Park
Chicago
Elmhurst
290
Cicero
El. 597 ft.
Wheaton
41
Batavia
Aurora
TOLL
Naper
ville
55
Oak Lawn
90
Whiting
E. Chicago
Bolingbrook
Harvey
Hammond
Ogden
Orland
Park
Gary
Plainfield
Park
Highland
Hobart
For
Munster
Merrillville
Joliet
New Frankfort
30
Chicago
Hts
52
WILL
Park
Univ.
Pkg.
St. John
253
Valpa
Crown
Point
247
741
Elwood
221
Goodenow
INDIANA
Cedar
Lake
Leroy
Hebron
Peotone
Beecher
41
Diamond
Wilmington
Lowell
740
Braidwood
45
Momence
Schneider
230
Essex
315
Sun River Terrace
Lake
Village
312
Kankakee
KANKAKEE
65
Dwight
Reddick
Aroma
Park
Herscher
Park
Lenox
Campus
Cabery
Chebanse
302
297
Papineau
Morocco
Rens
Stelle
174
Kempton
Martinton
Ravenne
215
Cullom
45
57
Brook
16
Ashkum
Iroquois
Charlotte
Piper
Danforth
City
Kentland
Forrest
Crescent
Watseka
24
City
Sheldon
Chatsworth
IROQUOIS
Onarga
Woodland
71
Strawn
Milford
Stockland
Roberts
Dawson
Park
Sibley
Buckley
Goodwine
Melvin
Cissna
Wellington
FORD
Park
Boswe

> **Everything
> in life is
> someplace
> else, and
> you get
> there in a
> car.**
>
> E. B. White

CRUISE CONTROL

	1	2	3	4	5	6	7	8	9	10

DESTINATION   **DATE**

A

                                   MILEAGE

B

C

D

E

F

G

H

I

J

K

L

M

N

O

DESTINATION   DATE

                                    MILEAGE

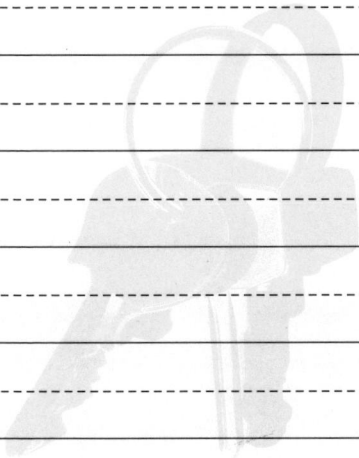

Sometimes the miles just disappear but sometimes you have to drive every single one of them.

Graham Coster

	1	2	3	4	5	6	7	8	9	10

DESTINATION   **DATE**

A

                                   MILEAGE

B

C

D

E

F

G

H

I

J

K

L

M

N

O

| 11 | 12 | 13 | 14 | 15 | 16 | 17 | 18 | 19 | 20 |

DESTINATION   **DATE**

A

                                                        MILEAGE

B

C

D

E

F

G

H

I

> Journeys, like artists, are born and not made. A thousand differing circumstances contribute to them, few of them willed or determined by the will—whatever we may think.
>
> Laurence Durrell

J

K

L

M

N

O

DESTINATION

DATE

MILEAGE

A sign
along the
side of the
highway
says "Just
ahead: see
albino
racoon."
I put my
foot on the
brake.

Calvin Trillin

| | 1 | 2 | 3 | 4 | 5 | 6 | 7 | 8 | 9 | 10 |

DESTINATION

DATE

MILEAGE

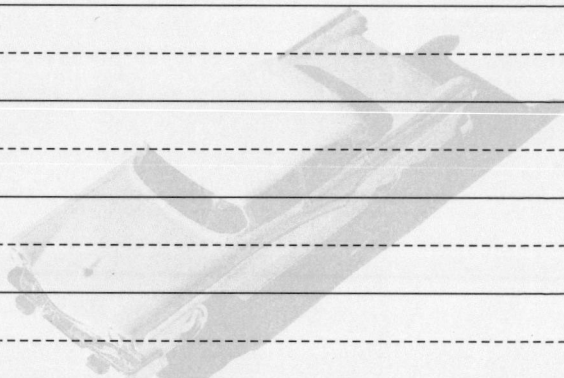

A
B
C
D
E
F
G
H
I
J
K
L
M
N
O

| 11 | 12 | 13 | 14 | 15 | 16 | 17 | 18 | 19 | 20 |

DESTINATION

DATE

MILEAGE

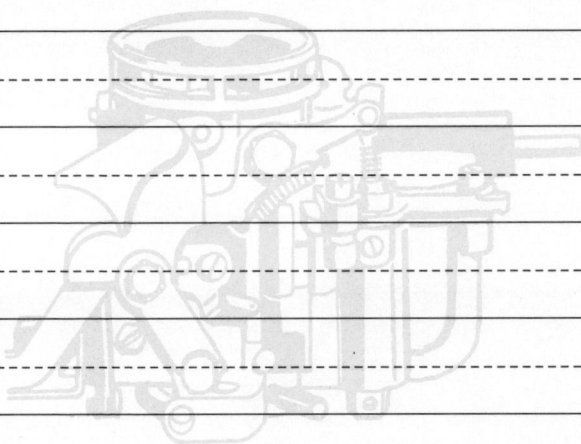

A journey
is best
measured
in friends
rather
than
miles.

Tim Cahill

	1	2	3	4	5	6	7	8	9	10

DESTINATION   **DATE**

MILEAGE

A

B

C

D

E

F

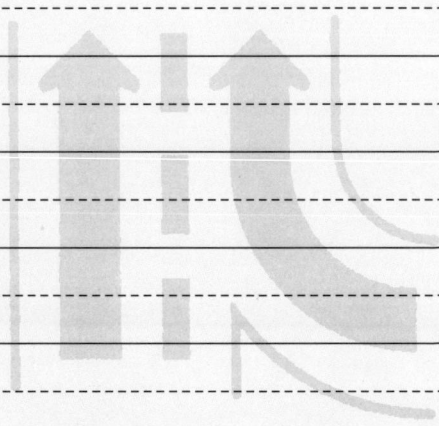

G

H

I

J

K

L

M

N

O

| 11 | 12 | 13 | 14 | 15 | 16 | 17 | 18 | 19 | 20 |

DESTINATION

DATE

MILEAGE

The sky breaks like an egg into full sunset and the water caught fire.

Pamela Hansford Johnson

	1	2	3	4	5	6	7	8	9	10

DESTINATION

DATE

MILEAGE

A

B

C

D

E

F

G

H

I

J

K

L

M

N

O

DESTINATION _____ DATE _____

MILEAGE _____

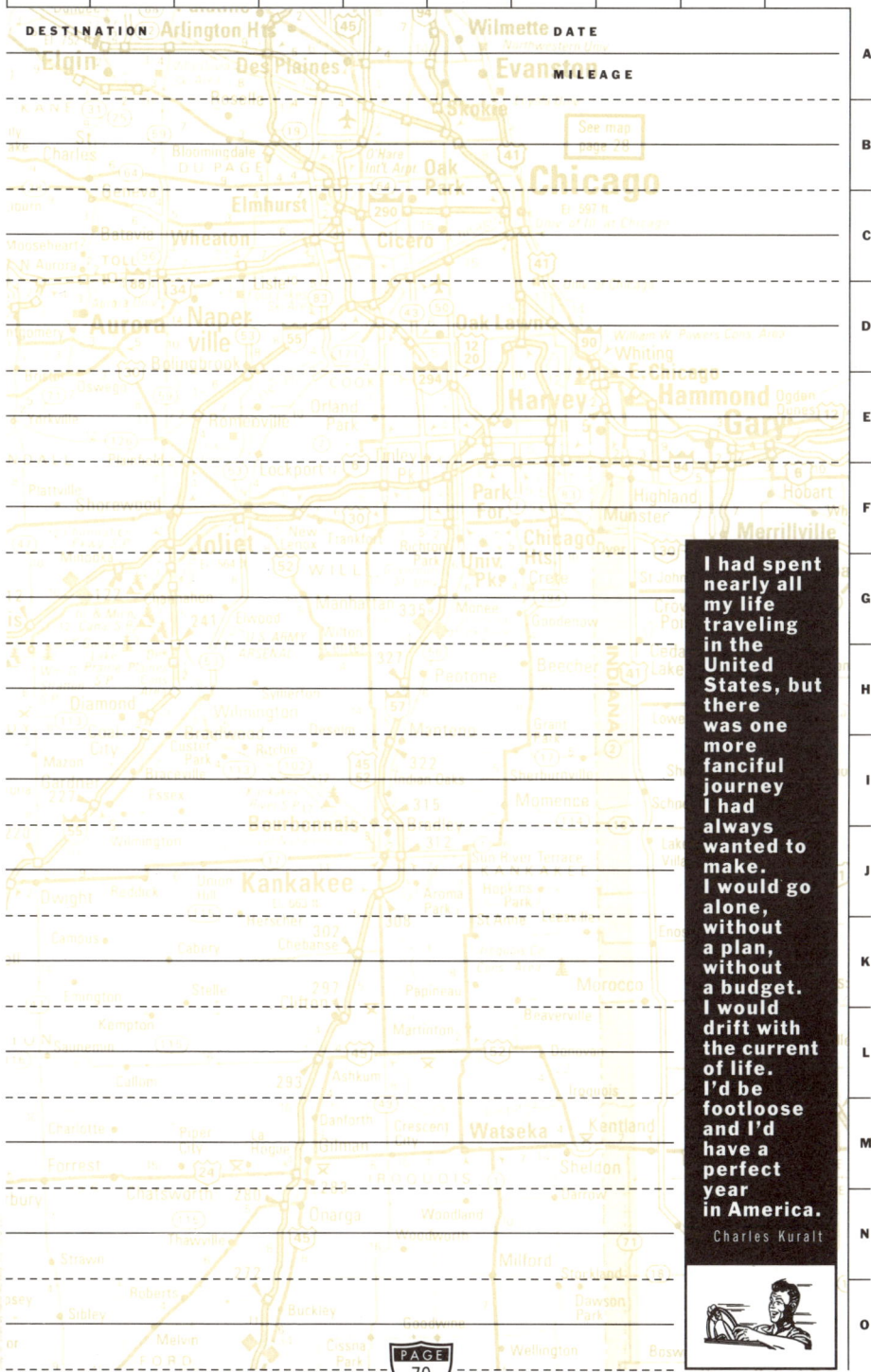

> I had spent nearly all my life traveling in the United States, but there was one more fanciful journey I had always wanted to make. I would go alone, without a plan, without a budget. I would drift with the current of life. I'd be footloose and I'd have a perfect year in America.
>
> Charles Kuralt

	1	2	3	4	5	6	7	8	9	10

DESTINATION

DATE

MILEAGE

A

B

C

D

E

F

G

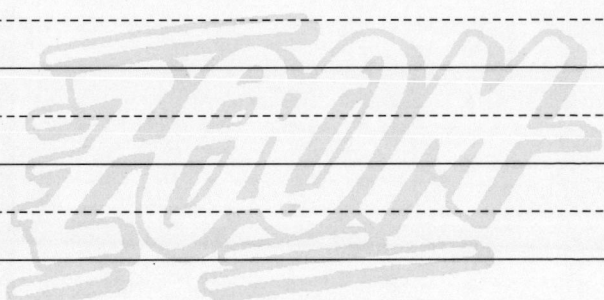

H

I

J

K

L

M

N

O

DESTINATION   **DATE**

                                                       MILEAGE

A

B

C

D

E

F

G

H

I

J

K

L

M

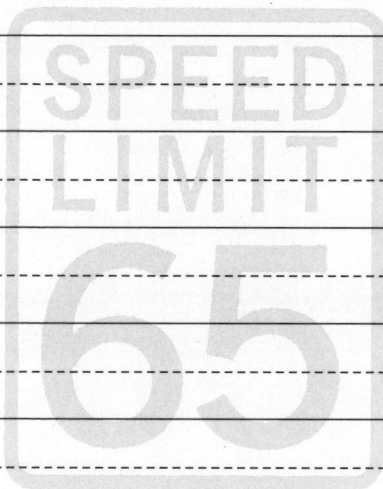

**66 is
the mother
road.**

John Steinbeck

N

O

	1	2	3	4	5	6	7	8	9	10
A	**DESTINATION**						**DATE**			
							MILEAGE			
B										
C										
D										
E										
F										
G										
H										
I										
J										
K										
L										
M										
N										
O										

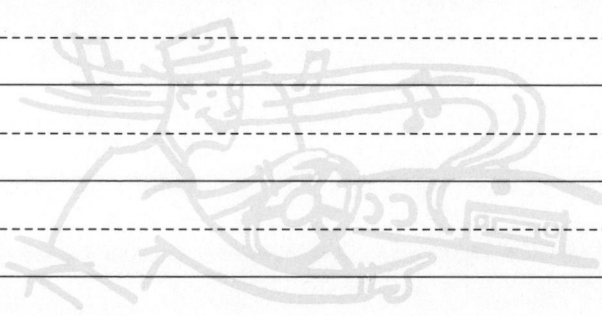

| 11 | 12 | 13 | 14 | 15 | 16 | 17 | 18 | 19 | 20 |

DESTINATION

DATE

MILEAGE

The Mississippi meanders down the spine of America.

Bob Dodson

DESTINATION **DATE**

MILEAGE

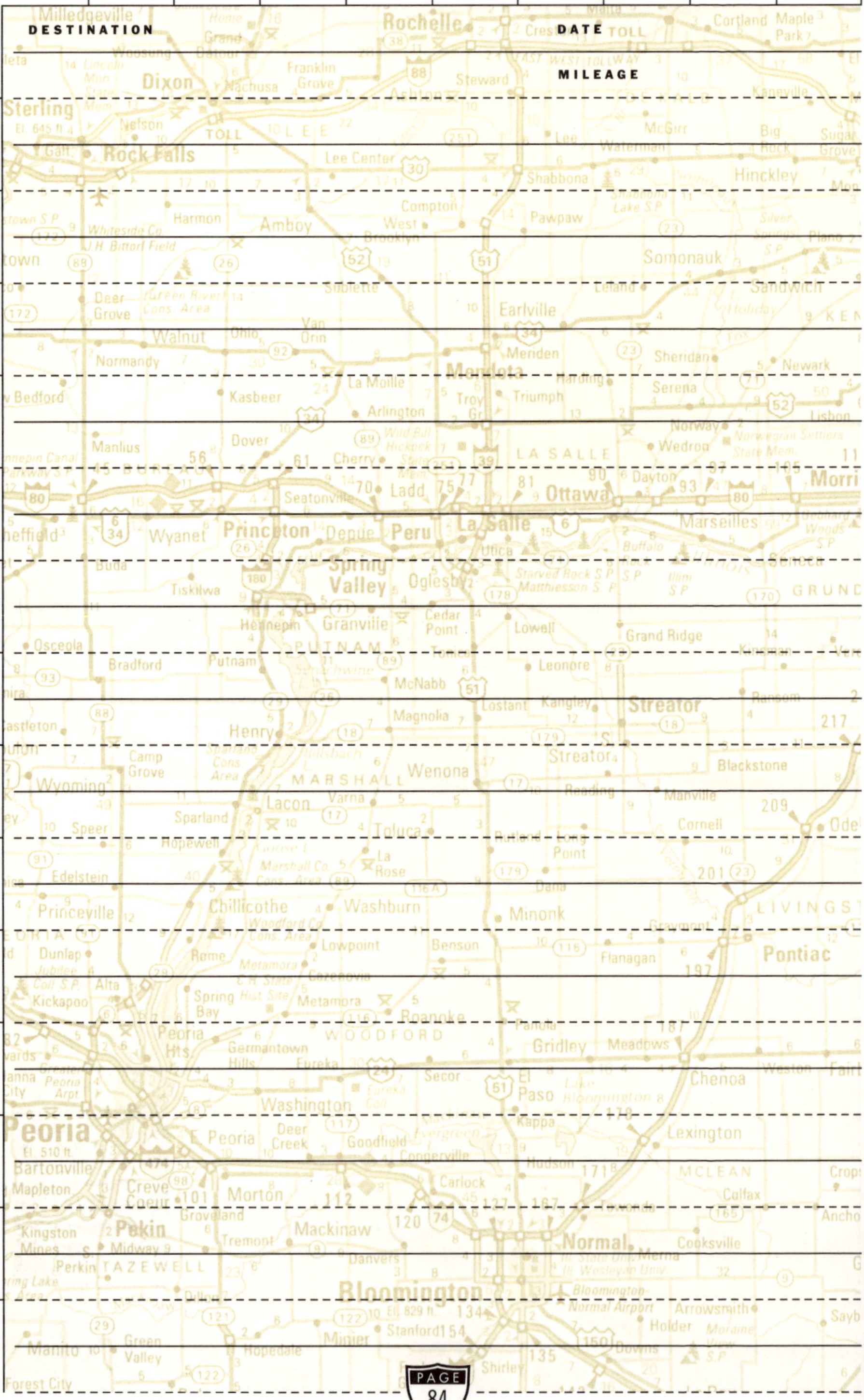

| 11 | 12 | 13 | 14 | 15 | 16 | 17 | 18 | 19 | 20 |

DESTINATION   **DATE**

MILEAGE

The great
home of
the soul is
the Open
Road. Not
heaven,
not
paradise.
Not
"above."
Not even
"within."
It is a
wayfarer
down the
road.

D.H. Lawrence

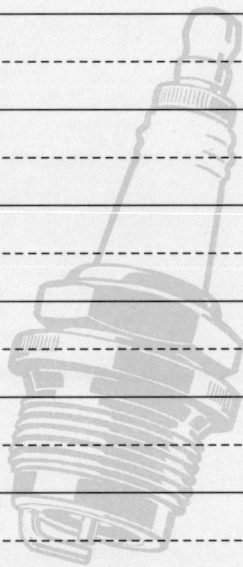

	1	2	3	4	5	6	7	8	9	10

DESTINATION   **DATE**

MILEAGE

A
B
C
D
E
F
G
H
I
J
K
L
M
N
O

| 11 | 12 | 13 | 14 | 15 | 16 | 17 | 18 | 19 | 20 |

DESTINATION

DATE

MILEAGE

> On the road again, goin' places that I've never been, seein' things that I may never see again, I can't wait to get on the road again.
> — Willie Nelson

THE Grand TOURER

FREEWAY ENTRANCE

	1	2	3	4	5	6	7	8	9	10

DESTINATION

DATE

MILEAGE

A

B

C

D

E

F

G

H

I

J

K

L

M

N

O

11	12	13	14	15	16	17	18	19	20

DESTINATION

DATE

MILEAGE

A
B
C
D
E
F
G
H
I

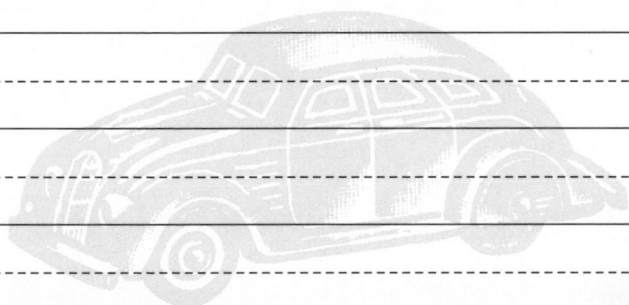

J
K
L
M
N
O

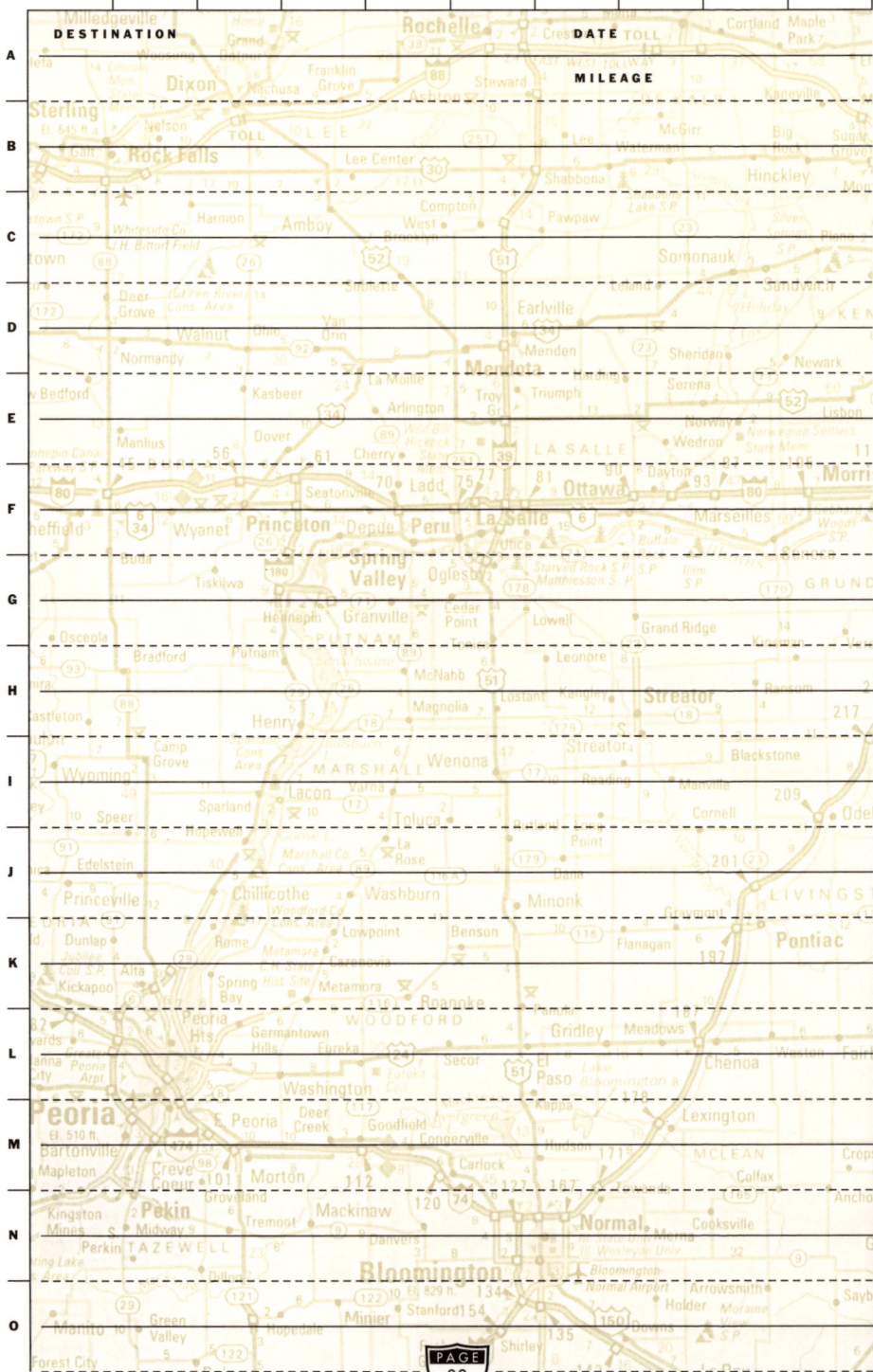

DESTINATION **DATE** TOLL

MILEAGE

DESTINATION

DATE

MILEAGE

A
B
C
D
E
F
G
H
I
J
K
L
M
N
O

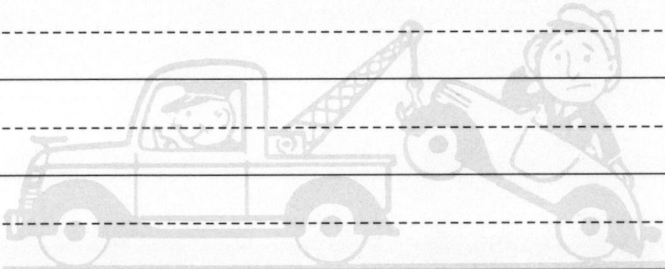

You're
either on
the bus
or off the
bus.

Ken Kesey

	1	2	3	4	5	6	7	8	9	10

DESTINATION **DATE**

MILEAGE

A

B

C

D

E

F

G

H

I

J

K

L

M

N

O

DESTINATION

DATE

MILEAGE

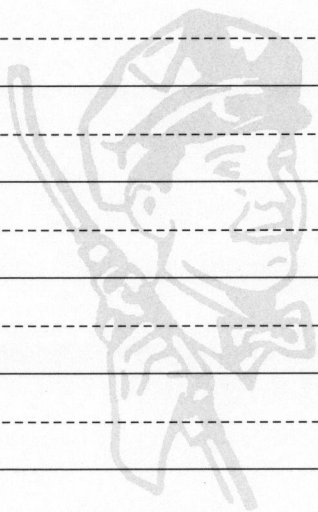

> I think that cars today are almost the exact equivalent of the great Gothic cathedrals: I mean the supreme creation of an era, conceived with passion by unknown artists, and consumed in image if not in usage by a whole population which appropriates them as a purely magical object.
>
> Roland Barthes

	1	2	3	4	5	6	7	8	9	10

DESTINATION   **DATE**

                                          MILEAGE

A — B — C — D — E — F — G — H — I — J — K — L — M — N — O

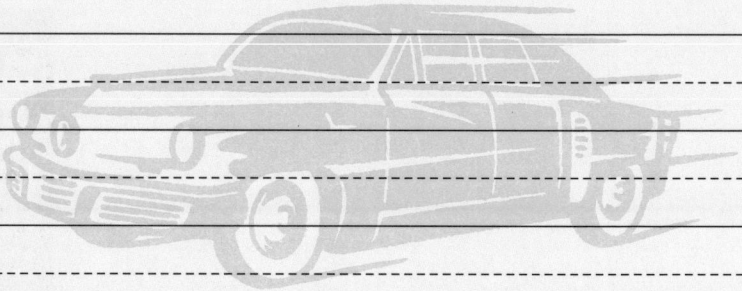

11	12	13	14	15	16	17	18	19	20

DESTINATION   **DATE**

A

MILEAGE

B

C

D

E

F

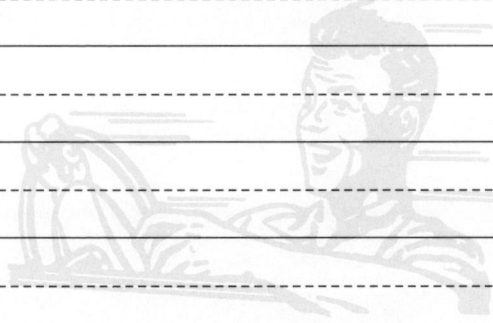

G

H

I

J

K

L

M

N

O

The road's
what
counts.
Don't
worry
about
where it's
goin'.

Sam Shepard

FIVE SPEED

TRANSMISSION

	1	2	3	4	5	6	7	8	9	10

DESTINATION   **DATE**

MILEAGE

A

B

C

D

E

F

G

H

I

J

K

L

M

N

O

Cruising through the countryside in my monkmobile, listening to Bach, munching on cellophane snacks, provided me a space and time machine of incredible capacity.

Abbot Benedict OSB

	1	2	3	4	5	6	7	8	9	10

DESTINATION

DATE

MILEAGE

A

B

C

D

E

F

G

H

I

J

K

L

M

N

O

11	12	13	14	15	16	17	18	19	20

DESTINATION   **DATE**

                                                    MILEAGE

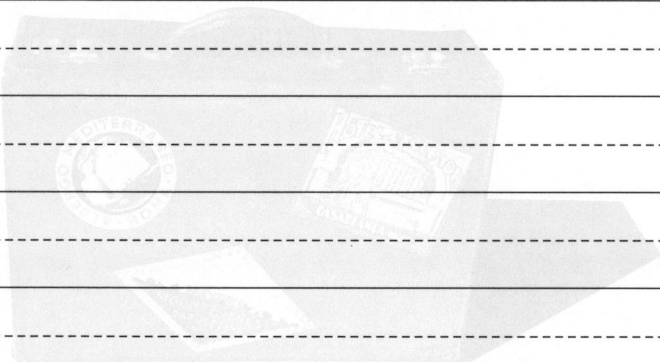

A

B

C

D

E

F

G

H

I

J

K

L

Whither goest thou, America, in thy shiny car in the night.

Jack Kerouac

M

N

O

	1	2	3	4	5	6	7	8	9	10

DESTINATION　　　　　　　　　　　**DATE**

　　　　　　　　　　　　　　　　　　　MILEAGE

CRUISE CONTROL

| 11 | 12 | 13 | 14 | 15 | 16 | 17 | 18 | 19 | 20 |

DESTINATION   **DATE**

A

MILEAGE

B

C

D

E

F

G

H

I

J

K

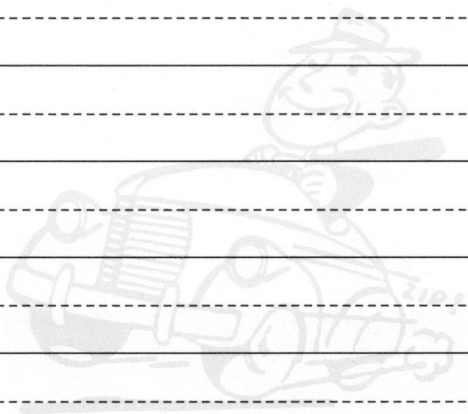

> Into the
> great wide
> open
> under the
> skies of
> blue, out
> in the
> great wide
> open
> a rebel
> without
> a clue.
>
> Tom Petty

L

M

N

O

DESTINATION

DATE

MILEAGE

A

B

C

D

E

F

G

H

I

J

K

L

M

N

O

I been a
wanderin'
Early and
late,
New York
City
To the
Golden
Gate
An' it
looks like
I'm never
gonna
cease my
Wanderin'.

Carl Sandburg

	1	2	3	4	5	6	7	8	9	10

DESTINATION　　　　　　　　　　　　　**DATE**

MILEAGE

A

B

C

D

E

F

G

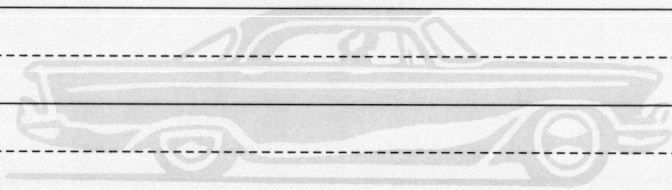

H

I

J

K

L

M

N

O

| 11 | 12 | 13 | 14 | 15 | 16 | 17 | 18 | 19 | 20 |

DESTINATION

DATE

MILEAGE

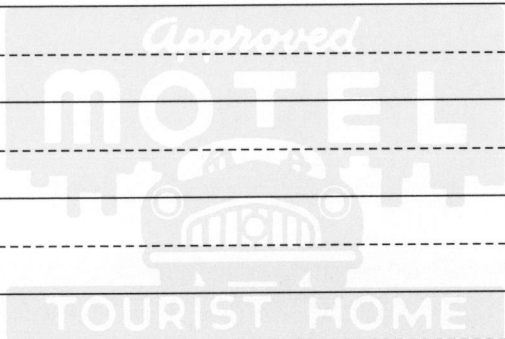

A perfect
experience
in the
perfect
momentum
set
perfectly
by his foot
on the
accelerator.

Tom Wolfe

	1	2	3	4	5	6	7	8	9	10

DESTINATION　　　　　　　　　　　　　　**DATE**

MILEAGE

A
B
C
D
E
F
G
H
I
J
K
L
M
N
O

11	12	13	14	15	16	17	18	19	20

DESTINATION

DATE

MILEAGE

A

B

C

D

E

F

G

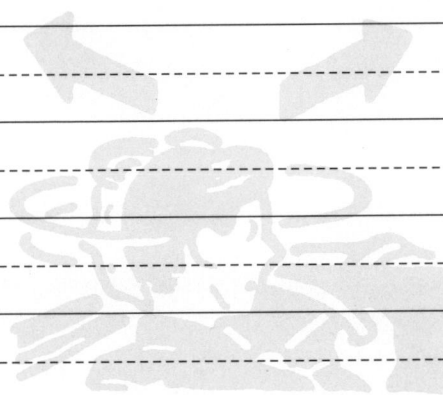

H

> **Open-road travelers are made more than born. They are as different from theme-park tourists as anything you can imagine. Tourists rush; travelers mosey. Tourists want to see all the right places; travelers simply go into the country.**
>
> Tom Snyder

I

J

K

L

M

N

O

DESTINATION

DATE

MILEAGE

A
B
C
D
E
F
G
H

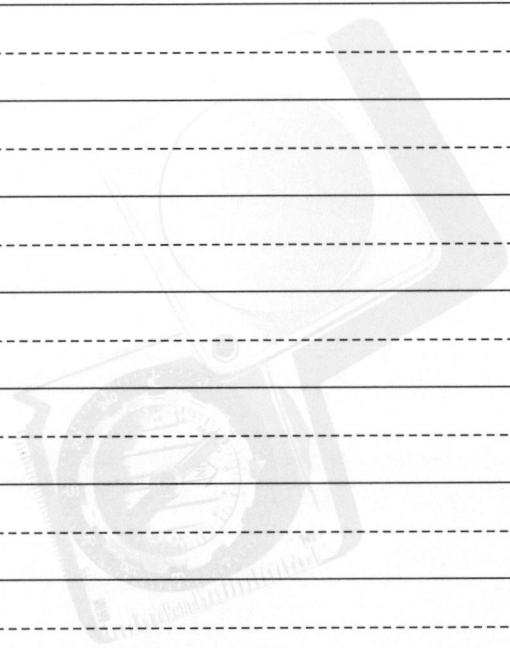

A peril of
the night
road is
that flecks
of dust
and
streaks of
bug blood
on the
windshield
look to me
like old
admirals
in uniform
or the
front edge
of barges,
and I whirl
out of
their way,
thus going
into
ditches
and fields
or up on
front
lawns.

James Thurber

I
J
K
L
M
N
O

	1	2	3	4	5	6	7	8	9	10

DESTINATION

DATE

MILEAGE

A

B

C

D

E

F

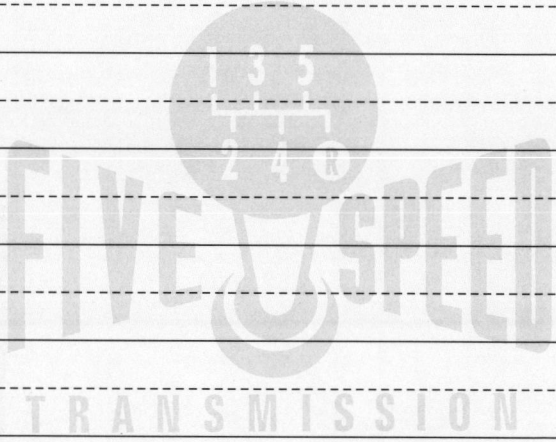

G

H

I

J

K

L

M

N

O

| 11 | 12 | 13 | 14 | 15 | 16 | 17 | 18 | 19 | 20 |

DESTINATION

DATE

MILEAGE

> I only care
> to splitly
> down to
> my old '55.
> I pulled
> away
> slowly,
> God knows
> I was
> feelin'
> alive.
>
> — Tom Waits

SPEED LIMIT 65

	1	2	3	4	5	6	7	8	9	10

DESTINATION

DATE

MILEAGE

DESTINATION

DATE

MILEAGE

A
B
C
D
E
F
G
H
I
J
K
L
M
N
O

Speed Meter

2005215

Hop in your car and drive in any direction for five hours, at any speed on any highway or road, with no objective, no one to meet, alone behind the wheel. Then, when the tank nears empty, fuel up at a gas station, look into the sky, feel the wind, sun, rain, or snow in your face, and freedom is yours.

Douglas Brinkley

	1	2	3	4	5	6	7	8	9	10

DESTINATION　　　　　　　　　　　　　**DATE**

MILEAGE

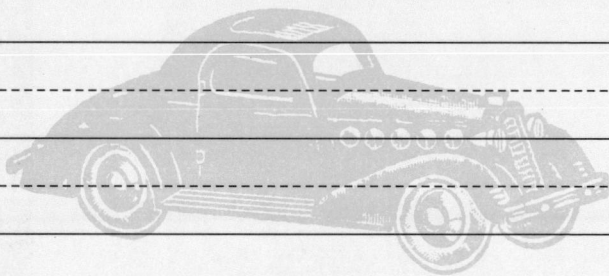

A

B

C

D

E

F

G

H

I

J

K

L

M

N

O

WITHOUT MUSIC, A ROAD TRIP IS JUST ANOTHER TREK FROM POINT A TO POINT B. MUSIC GREASES THE WHEELS OF YOUR MIND. IT'S THE RHYTHMIC ENGINE THAT PROPELS YOU UP SKY-TOPPED PEAKS, INSPIRES OPERATIC EFFORTS ON LONG, LONELY STRETCHES OF HIGHWAY, AND SETTLES YOU BACK AGAINST YOUR SEAT WHILE CRUISING THROUGH ROLLING VALLEYS. MUSIC ALSO IS A WELCOME COMPANION, SPEAKING ONLY WHEN SPOKEN TO AND KEEPING YOU GOING WHEN STUCK IN RADIO WASTELAND. FOLLOWING ARE SOME TUNES THAT WILL GET YOUR MOTOR RUNNING:

AMERICA Simon and Garfunkel clamber aboard a Greyhound with friend Kathy in search of America. Easy listening and shades of the past.

BORN TO BE WILD If you're feeling devil may care, Steppenwolf will take you where you want to go. "Lookin' for adventure and whatever comes our way." Need we say more?

COWBOY ROMANCE Natalie Merchant's cowboy boyfriend invites her to come away with him and "be drifters free." A moody ballad about a relationship going nowhere.

DRIVE MY CAR Let's see: she wants to be famous, a star on the screen, while his prospects are good. Hard to tell who's behind the wheel in this Beatles number.

FLOORBOARD BLUES Cowboy Junkies lead singer Margo Simmons, hitching her way across country, says "no" to a ride with a guy driving a beat up Rambler with Nebraska plates and sporting a pinky ring. Sounds like she used good judgment.

FREEWAY OF LOVE The Queen of Soul Aretha Franklin leaves the Motor City behind, to go ridin' on the freeway of love in her pink Cadillac. Can you drive and dance at the same time?

GRACELAND If Elvis's homestead isn't on your itinerary, this Paul Simon chartbuster will make you reconsider. Tap out the rhythm on your steering wheel and sing along.

I'M A TRAVELIN' MAN As he journeys around the world, Ricky Nelson wins the heart of "at least one lovely girl" in every port he visits. What a day for a daydream.

LITTLE GTO There's nothing like California surfer music to rev your engine. By the time the Beach Boys stop singing, you've got the pedal to the medal and have settled into your cruising speed.

MERCEDES BENZ A laughing little ditty from Janis Joplin, this tune is fun to include even if a Mercedes isn't your idea of a dream car.

MAYBELLINE Motorvatin' along in his V8 Ford, Chuck Berry spies Maybelline and a coup de ville movin' on an open road. The rest is rock and roll history. Great tune for making good time.

NO MONEY DOWN Blues guitarist John Hammond trades in his broken-down, ragged Ford for a Cadillac—what else? Not just any Cadillac: a yellow convertible with a TV and phone, air conditioning, and a roll-away bed in the backseat. Hard to find but worth it.

ON THE ROAD AGAIN Self-proclaimed nomad Willie Nelson is happiest when he's on the road with his band, seein' things he may never see again and goin' place he's never been. Definitely an inspiration.

REFUGE OF THE ROADS Joni Mitchell leaves her boyfriend behind for a world of drifters, Winn Dixie coldcuts and cold water restrooms as she travels west trying to lose herself on the road. Is that what awaits you?

RIDE OF THE VALKYRIES When you need a horsepower jolt, this Wagner composition (it's classical so "song" seems banal) will help you scale the highest mountains or eat up miles of straight, empty road. Anyone have a baton?

ROUTE 66 A pop standard that takes you from Chicago to L.A. along one of America's most famous highways. The Rolling Stones did a down and funky rock version, but try the Nat King Cole Trio jazz rendition for a change of pace.

TAKE IT EASY The Eagles may have seven women on their minds as they're runnin' down the road, but they're still lookin' for a lover who won't blow their cover. Another sing along tune.

THE DRIVING SONG With its driving blues baseline and signature flute, this Jethro Tull number is a great blast from the past. A plaintive tale of a need for rest if "I'm gonna do my best," it asks "Can I be by myself?" The answer: yes.

THE RIDE Country-western tale-spinner David Allen Coe sings of the time he was hitching to Nashville and was picked up by the great Hank Williams, "dressed like 1950 in an antique Cadillac," who offers sage advice about fame. Shades of Howard Hughes.

THE WING AND THE WHEEL Country songstress Nanci Griffith will ease your mind with this ballad about how the wheel and wings of love carry all the dreamers away—herself included. A tune everyone can relate to.

THUNDER ROAD Bruce Springsteen sings of his last chance at redemption and to make it real with his girl Mary. One of his first big hits, Springsteen admits he "stole" the title from a Robert Mitchum movie and the vocal sound from Roy Orbison.

TRUCKIN' Tired of traveling and performing in a different place night after night, the Grateful Dead sing about "what a long strange trip it's been." A mellow sing along when you're taking your time.

WANDERER Dion, formerly with the Belmonts, just can't seem to settle down. He's never in one place, just roams from town to town. Who knows what's down the road?

IT'S A WIDELY ACCEPTED TRUTH THAT TRAVEL BROADENS THE MIND.
HOWEVER, MOBILIZING YOURSELF IS NOT ALWAYS POSSIBLE. HERE ARE SOME
EXCURSIONS YOU CAN IMMERSE YOURSELF IN WITHOUT LEAVING YOUR
ARMCHAIR. THEY'LL GET YOU AWAY FROM IT ALL AS YOU VICARIOUSLY SAVOR
THE EXPERIENCES RELIVED BY THE AUTHORS IN THEIR WRITINGS.

A THOUSAND MILES FROM NOWHERE: TRUCKING TWO CONTINENTS
Graham Coster, North Point Press, 1995. Graham Coster crisscrosses North America and
Europe with men who drive diesel rigs thousands of miles at a stretch and call their
sleeper cabs home. In Europe he ventures out with an English long-hauler who's carrying
ice cream and Guiness to Russia. In the United States, he accompanies a string of colorful
characters who view themselves as late 20th Century cowboys. As he motors along, vast
expanses of land spread before him, Coster finds the mythology of the open road as
seductive as ever.

A TRIP TO THE LIGHT FANTASTIC: TRAVELS WITH A MEXICAN CIRCUS
Katie Hickman, Flamingo, 1994. A member of England's Wanderlust Club, Katie Hickman
traveled to Mexico in search of a magical adventure. Inspired by intriguing tales recounted
by the daughter of a circus family, Hickman sets off to find her own big-top experience. She
joins Circo Bell's: El Circo Mas Famosa en Toda Las Americas, a nomadic lifestyle to which
she quickly adjusts. Hickman tells of being caught up in a hypnotic world where cheap torn
materials and tarnished sequins are transformed into nights of glittering illusion, and of
belonging to a fantastic family of characters such as Olga, who was struck dumb by the
1985 Mexico City earthquake, then rescued from silence by the love of a prize fighter. This
is the story of her epic, year-long journey in which she metamorphoses from foreigner into
"Las Gringa Estrella," a performer in her own right.

A YEAR IN PROVENCE
Peter Mayle, Vantage Books, 1991. Peter Mayle takes you along as he realizes a long-
cherished dream: to actually move into a 200-year-old stone farmhouse in the remote
region of the Luberon with his wife and two large dogs. With him, you share the earthly
pleasures of Provençal life and live vicariously at a tempo governed by seasons, not days.

CHARLES KURALT'S AMERICA
Charles Kuralt, G.P. Putnam's Sons, 1995. One of the U.S.'s premier chroniclers, Charles
Kuralt retired from CBS News and set off to revisit many of the people and places he'd
reported on during his nearly 30 years with the network. Laced with warmth, humor, and
uncommon insight, the book takes you to Montana in summer, Alaska in June, deep into
Cajun country in winter, and through the North Carolina mountains in spring.

ELECTRIC KOOL-AID ACID TEST

Tom Wolfe, Farrar, Straus and Giroux, 1968. Intrigued by Ken Kesey's transformation from Golden Boy novelist to criminal on the run, journalist-raconteur Tom Wolfe sallies forth to find Kesey and do a story on Young Novelist Real-Life Fugitive. In the process, Wolfe joins "The Chief" and his band of Merry Pranksters for an altered-states sojourn around the U.S. aboard a psychedelic bus. It is a wild and zany romp that finds them busting in on Timothy Leary and his League for Spiritual Discovery in Millbrook, New York, accompanying Kesey to a lecture at Esalen, playing hide-and-seek from the law in Mexico, and evolving from a loose-knit commune into a new religion.

FALLING OFF THE MAP: SOME LONELY PLACES OF THE WORLD

Pico Iyer, Vintage Books, 1994. Seeking a different kind of adventure, Pico Iyer sets out in search of lonely places, places he defines as cut off from the rest of the world by geography, ideology, or sheer weirdness. Travel with him as he explores such destinations as Cuba, the island no one thinks of as West Indian; Iceland, the island that isn't really part of Europe; Australia, an island no one knows whether to call an island or a continent, as well as the off-the-beaten-path territories of North Korea, Argentina, Bhutan, Vietnam, and Paraguay.

MOTEL NIRVANA: DREAMING OF THE NEW AGE IN THE AMERICAN DESERT

Melanie McGrath, Picador USA, 1995. Seeking an American spiritual journey, McGrath leaves Britain behind to spend two seasons motoring through new age communities in New Mexico, Nevada, Arizona, Utah, and Colorado. In her 13,000-mile trek, she meets a Jesus channeler, camps out at love-ins, and stays in a house owned by a family of aliens from the constellation Pleiades. With a razor-sharp wit, McGrath writes about attending a "knowing" in New Mexico with people who gather "knowing" from themselves and "apply it to a place of enlightenment," and about sharing a luxury Arizona hotel with an Italian prince who thinks he will never die.

ON PERSEPHONE'S ISLAND: A SICILIAN JOURNEY

Mary Taylor Simetti, First Vintage, 1986. Brooklyn-born Mary Taylor Simetti sets off for what she lovingly calls Persephone's Island (for the goddess who once made Sicily her home), intending to stay for a short visit. Instead, Simonetti falls in love with its people, food, and traditions, remaining there for more than 20 years. We accompany her as she explores the history of the Greek, Arab, Norman, and Spanish conquests of this culture-rich island, attends such festivals as the feast of Aphrodite Erycina, and savors the delectable fruits of Sicily's harvests.

ON THE ROAD

Jack Kerouac, Penguin Books, 1991. The definitive novel from the Beat Generation, Kerouac's masterpiece transports you through underground America of the fifties. Sail down highways and backroads with Sal Paradise and his hero Dean Moriarty as they relive their childhoods and grab hold of a life unencumbered by societal mores and restrictions.

POLAR DREAM

Helen Thayer, Bantam Doubleday Dell, 1993. In 1988, Helen Thayer embarked on a journey never before attempted by a woman: to ski to the North Pole. Thayer planned to make the trip alone, until she was persuaded at the last minute to take along a black husky she named Charlie. She was glad she did. The first and best warning of impending polar bear attacks, Charlie hurled himself into a bear's path when Thayer's gun was not enough. Later, caught in a biting snowstorm with temperatures of minus 33°, Charlie leads the nearly blinded and frozen Thayer across a landscape of cliffs, ice pinnacles, and howling winds to the North Pole.

ROAD FEVER: A HIGH-SPEED TRAVELOGUE
Tim Cahill, Vintage Books, 1991. Tim Cahill breaks through the distance/time barrier as he whips his car along a 15,000 mile marathon that starts in Tierra del Fuego and ends in Prudhoe Bay Alaska in a mind-numbing 23½ days. In his quest to see how far he can go and how quickly, he encounters engine trouble in Patagonia, sadistic troopers in Peru, grueling hours of red-tape in Colombia, and ice-coated highways in Alaska. Cahill documents this epic road trip in a blood-racing style that leaves you laughing and breathless.

THE MAGIC BUS: AN AMERICAN ODYSSEY
Douglas Brinkley, Anchor Books, 1994. Challenged by his students to teach them American history outside the classroom, Hofstra University professor Douglas Brinkley devises a six-week on-the-road course that takes them from one end of the country to the other. Transported by Frank Perugi, the self-proclaimed "Buffalo Bill of Busing," aboard his "Magic Bus" (named for The Who's song), Brinkley and his entourage pay their respects at Martin Luther King Jr.'s Ebenezer Baptist Church in Atlanta, contemplate Robert Rauschenberg, Michael Jordan, and Gino's pizza in Chicago, spend two days at the Jack Kerouac School of Disembodied Poets in Boulder, Colorado, and pray with a Crow medicine man in Montana. The rhythms of their odyssey are those of Joni Mitchell, Frank Sinatra, the Sex Pistols, Patti Smith, Dixieland Jazz, Son Seals, Elvis Presley, and Bob Dylan.

TRAVELS
Michael Crichton, Ballantine, 1988. Michael Crichton, author of *Jurassic Park*, fueled by a voracious appetite for adventure, voyages into worlds as diverse and compelling as those he creates in his popular novels. Pushed by a need to see, feel, and hear first-hand and up close, he continuously seeks out ways to test himself and, in the process, his spirituality. Such pursuits take him to the jungles of Pahong in Malaysia and a late-night encounter with an elephant in Kenya. *Travels* is just the ticket for those who want to escape and to know risk for perhaps the first time.

TUMMY TRILOGY
Calvin Trillin, The Noonday Press, 1994. As a *New Yorker* columnist, Calvin Trillin traveled around the United States from 1972-1982, writing about America without concentrating on its government or politics. Instead, he focused on how a traveler in a strange city goes about finding something decent to eat. Shunning places "over a hundred feet off the ground" and which "won't stand still," Trillin offers suggestions for finding the best local restaurants. His pearls of culinary wisdom include such sage advice as "if a barbecue restaurant serves on plates, try someplace else."

OKAY, YOUR SUITCASES ARE PACKED, THE TANK'S FULL, THE OIL'S CHECKED,
AND THE BRAKES ARE RELINED. TIME TO GO. BUT BEFORE YOU TAKE OFF, YOU MAY WANT TO BRING
ALONG SOME ESSENTIAL ITEMS THAT EVERY WELL-PREPARED NOMAD ALWAYS CARRIES.

JACK Stuck on a back road with a flat tire and no other vehicles in sight? You'll be glad you remembered to take this little tool.

TOOL KIT Speaking of tools, you never know when a screwdriver, hammer, or wrench will come in handy.

EXTRA CAN OF OIL It's always a good idea to have at least one can stowed away for emergencies.

FIRST AID KIT The need for this item is pretty obvious. Make sure your kit is stocked with tape and bandages as well as band-aids for small cuts and scrapes. And don't forget the iodine and cotton balls. Better safe than sorry.

FLARES No one wants to think about car trouble on the road, but stuff happens. Toss some flares into your trunk in case you need to flag down help or warn oncoming motorists of your existence.

FLASHLIGHT Reading the tiny print of road-maps, fixing a flat or searching for items that fell out of the car are difficult enough during the day and an even bigger challenge at night. Be sure to tuck a flashlight and some extra batteries under your seat.

JUMPER CABLES On the off chance that you leave your lights on or your battery weakens inexplicably, you want to make sure you carry a set of these—the longer the cables the better.

PAPER AND PEN When asking for directions, paper and pen come in very handy. They're also good for jotting down phone numbers, addresses and other info you may need later.

A GOOD SELECTION OF TAPES OR CDS Don't count on the radio to keep you trucking along. You may hit some places with no reception, or worse—how many songs can you listen to about broken relationships?

BOTTLE OPENER The pause that refreshes won't if you don't have any way of opening up the bottle.

CAN OPENER How about some crackers and smoked oysters for an afternoon respite. Have you ever tried to open a can with a knife?

UTENSILS No vehicle should be without at least one knife, fork, and spoon. They don't have to be metal, just functional.

BLANKET AND PILLOWS Necessary for a variety of occasions, a blanket and pillow make a little snooze under a tree more comfy —not to mention if you have to sleep in the car.

SOAP AND TOWELS Feeling drowsy or just want to wash road dust off your face? Not every restroom or rest stop is well-equipped. You'll be glad you brought your own.

NOTES

NOTES

NOTES

NOTES

NOTES